iPhone 7

An Ultimate Walkthrough To The World's Latest iPhone Model

CONTENTS

INTRODUCTION

First and Foremost I want to thank you and congratulate you for downloading this iPhone 7 Guide Book

This book contains detailed instructions and strategies on how to get the best experience from your iPhone 7 and make the most out of it. iPhone 7, together with iPhone 7 Plus, was introduced on September 7, 2016. It was released on September 16, 2016. The overall design can be similar to iPhone 6s but iPhone 7 has new colors available and additional dust and water resistance. It also comes with earphones that connect using Lightning.

Thanks again for downloading this book, let's quickly get into it.

1

GETTING STARTED WITH IPHONE 7

After purchasing a brand new iPhone 7 or any other iPhones, the very first thing that you have to do is to set it up so that you can already use it right away. The start-up process includes going through "Hello" then adding your accounts such as Apple ID, Gmail, Yahoo Mail and others. In order to use FaceTime and iMessage to connect with your family and friends, you have to sign in with your Apple ID.

If you are still in the exploration mode to get to know your iPhone 7, there is no need to worry anymore. We can guide you through the whole process with tips and tricks on how to get things done easily so you can have the best experience with your iPhone 7.

Setting up iPhone 7

During the setup of your iPhone, you can start over anytime by simply pressing the Home button then tap Start Over.

1. Turn on your iPhone 7

When you buy a brand new iPhone 7 or any other iDevices, a simple "Hello" will greet you when you turn it on. It can also be in different languages. Press the **Home** button to start. For users with low vision, you can enable **VoiceOver** or **Zoom** right away. You can see your IMEI or MEID and ICCID by tapping the info icon "**i**" located in the lower right corner.

2. Select Your Country or Region

If you purchased your iPhone 7 in your country, it should already pick the right language. The country or region should also be right. Otherwise, choose your language then search for your country and region.

3. Choose a Wi-Fi Network and Enable Location Services

The next thing that will appear on your screen is **Choose a Wi-Fi Network** which allows you to connect to internet. If you already have an active service, you can select **Use Cellular Connection**. Otherwise, choose a Wi-Fi network.

After that, you get to decide whether you want to **Enable Location Services** or keep it disabled in the meantime. You can easily turn it on anytime when necessary.

4. Touch ID and Create a Passcode

Set up your **Touch ID** to allow your fingerprint to unlock your iPhone 7. For additional security, enter a six-digit passcode which you will need for features such as Apple Pay and Touch ID. You can tap

Passcode Options if you prefer four-digit, no passcode or customized passcode.

5. Apps & Data

There are four options that will appear to continue your iPhone 7 set up.

- **Restore from iCloud Backup** – Tapping this allows you to retrieve your backup files in iCloud. Simply sign in with your Apple ID and enter your password for the purchases you made. Keep your device connected until the setup is finished. Your files saved in iCloud will automatically download to your iPhone 7 such as music, photos and apps.

- **Restore from iTunes Backup** – If you want to restore from iTunes backup, tap this option then connect your iPhone 7 to your computer via USB. Launch iTunes from your computer and select your device. Click Restore Backup and wait for the process to be completed.

- **Set up as new** – You can select this option if you did not own any iDevices before buying iPhone 7. This means that you will start using your iPhone 7 from scratch with its default settings.

- **Move Data from Android** – This option allows you to move your data and files from your Android devices.

How to Restore from iCloud Backup

First, you need to back up your old device in iCloud so you can transfer the backup files to your brand new iPhone 7. To make a backup on your previous device, follow these steps:

1. Make sure that your previous device is connected to Wi-Fi.
2. Open Settings app, tap iCloud and select Backup. Check if iCloud Backup is enabled.
3. Tap Back Up Now.

4. Keep your device connected to internet until the process is completed.

After backing up your previous device, you can now continue to Restore from iCloud Backup option.

1. Select Restore from iCloud Backup option.

Tap Restore from iCloud Backup from the Apps & Data screen then tap Next. Sign in to iCloud using your Apple ID and password.

2. Select Your Backup

Choose a backup and check if the date as well as the size is right. If you made purchases from App Store or iTunes with different Apple IDs, you will be required to log in to each. You can also skip if you do not remember the password by tapping "Don't have an Apple ID or forgot it."

3. Wait to Finish

Keep your iPhone 7 connected to Wi-Fi until the process is completed. Make sure that you also have enough battery life to prevent it from turning off.

This option allows you to transfer your music, photos, videos and apps saved in your iCloud.

How to Restore from iTunes Backup

First, you need to make a backup of your previous device in iTunes so you can transfer your data to your iPhone 7. To make an iTunes backup, follow these steps:

1. Connect your old device to your PC or Mac.
2. Launch **iTunes**. Make sure that you are running the latest version of iTunes.
3. Click your device.
4. Click **Back Up Now**. Wait for the process to finish. To check if the backup was successful, go to Preferences then click Devices. You will find

your device as well as the time and date the backup was created.

After making an iTunes backup of your previous device, you can now restore your iPhone 7 from iTunes backup.

1. **Select Restore from iTunes Backup.**

   From Apps & Data screen, select Restore from iTunes Backup then tap Next.

2. **Connect to iTunes**

   Connect your iPhone to your PC or Mac and launch iTunes. Select your device.

3. **Restore Backup**

   Click Restore Backup and choose a backup.

4. **Wait to Finish**

   Keep your device connected to your computer until the restore process is finished. As much as possible, keep your device connected to internet and charging to avoid battery low problems.

The Restore from iTunes Backup option allows you to transfer music, photos and apps.

How to Set Up As New

If this is your first iPhone and there is no need to transfer any data from any iDevices, simply follow these steps. First, you have to use your iCloud account.

1. **Tap Set Up As New**

   Under Apps & Data screen, select Set Up As New.

2. **Sign in with iCloud Apple ID**

   In order to use iCloud, iTunes and App Store, you need to sign in with your Apple ID. To sign in with your existing Apple ID, simply enter your email address and password. You can tap Use different Apple IDs for iCloud & iTunes if that is the set up that you want.

3. Create an Apple ID

You can create an Apple ID right away for free or you can tap Skip This Step if you wish to continue later. You can create an Apple ID anytime you want to from the Settings app.

4. Agree to Terms and Conditions

Tap Agree to Apple's Terms and Conditions. Tap again to confirm your agreement.

5. Set up Apple Pay and iCloud Keychain

If you signed in with your Apple ID, you will be prompted to set up iCloud Drive, Apple Pay as well as iCloud Keychain.

Apple Pay is the Apple's Touch ID-based option for payment while iCloud Keychain is for saving and syncing all your passwords from all your devices.

6. Set Up Siri

The next interface that will appear is Siri. You can Set Up Siri right away or you can choose to Turn On Siri Later.

7. Choose Your Click

You can select the way of how your Home button will respond whenever you press it. Simply try all three and choose your preferred option. Simply tap Next once you are done. You can also skip this step and customize your Home button click later.

8. Display Zoom

The last step is to choose how you want to view your iPhone 7. Zoomed view allows you to see bigger controls, apps and texts while the Standard option is the normal view.

Simply tap **Get Started** to start using your brand new iPhone 7.

How to Move Data from Android

Before you start, make sure that your Android device has Wi-Fi turned on. Connect your iPhone 7 and Android device in to power. Also check if your iOS device will have enough space for all the data that you wish to move from your Android device.

1. **Select Move Data from Android**

   Under Apps & Data screen, tap Move Data from Android option.

2. **Launch Move to iOS app**

   Open Move to iOS app on your Android device then tap Continue. Read and Agree to the terms and conditions the tap Next.

3. **Wait for Ten-digit of Six-digit Code**

   On your iPhone, tap Continue from Move from Android screen and wait for a code. If you received an alert on your Android device saying that the internet connection is weak, you can simply disregard it.

4. Enter the Code

Once you received your code, you can enter it on your Android device. Transfer Data screen will be displayed.

5. Select the Content

Choose the files you want to move from your Android device to your iPhone 7 then tap Next. A loading bar will appear on your iPhone and wait for it to be completed even if an alert on your Android tells you that the transfer is finished. Depending on the amount of your files, it may take some time.

You can transfer your photos and videos, messages, contact numbers, calendars, web bookmarks, email accounts and other apps available on both App Store and Google Play from your Android device to iOS.

6. Set Up

Once the loading bar is complete, tap Done from your Android and tap Continue on your iPhone. Follow the steps on your screen to finish.

Set Up Mail, Contacts and Calendars

You can easily set up your mail, contacts and calendars whether you are using iCloud, Gmail, Outlook or others.

❑ **iCloud Mail, Contacts and Calendars**

1. Open **Settings** app on your iPhone and tap **iCloud**.
2. Enter your existing iCloud email and password then tap **Sign In**.
3. If you want all your data to combine with your iCloud storage, tap **Merge**. If not, tap **Don't Merge**.

4. Tap the switches next to Mail, Contacts, Calendars and other apps you wish to sync. By default, iCloud's services are enabled.

❏ **Gmail, Google Calendar and Google Contacts on iPhone 7**

To add your Google account to your new device, go to Settings and tap Mail, or Contacts or Calendar. You can use the built-in iOS Mail app by following the steps below.

1. From your Home screen, open **Settings** app.
2. Select **Mail**, **Contacts** or **Calendar.**
3. Tap **Accounts** and select **Add Account**.
4. Tap **Google** and enter your log in information. Simply tap **Next** after completing each step.
5. Toggle on the switches next to all the Google services you wish to sync. If you have existing mail, calendars and contacts, you need to tap either **Keep on My Phone** or **Delete**.
6. Tap **Save** to finish.

❏ Outlook Mail, Contacts and Calendar

If you are using Microsoft Outlook, here is the step by step instruction to set up your mail, contacts and calendar.

1. Open **Settings** app.
2. Select **Mail**, **Contacts** or **Calendar**.
3. Tap **Accounts** and select **Add Account**.
4. Enter your Outlook username and password then tap **Sign In**.
5. Tap **Yes** to collect your information.
6. Toggle on the switches next to all services you want to enable.
7. Tap **Save** to finish.

iPhone automatically locks when the screen has not been touched for a minute or more. You can adjust the lock timing by going to Settings > Display & Brightness > Auto-Lock.

2

MESSAGES, FACETIME AND CAMERA

● **Message: Experience Excellent Messaging**

iMessage is the Apple's built-in Messaging app which allows you to send SMS, photos, videos, sound as well as location instantly. The Apple's latest version of operating system which is iOS 10 introduced more awesome features to make your messaging experience better. There are bubble effects that you can include in your messages such as invisible ink, slam, gentle and loud. You can also enjoy screen effects which are fireworks, confetti, balloons and lasers.

How to Add Bubble Effects on Messages

To use the effects on your messages, you need to tap the **up arrow** on the bottom of the screen or right next to your text message box.

1. Type your message.

2. Tap the **up arrow** for at least two seconds to bring you to awesome effects which are slam, loud, gentle and invisible ink.

3. You can check how the effects will appear by swiping up and down.

4. Tap the dot next to the name of the effect that you want to use.

5. Tap the **up arrow** to send your message with effect.

How to Add Screen Effects on Messages

To add screen effects, tap the up arrow for at least two seconds then swipe from Bubble to Screen. This will show you screen effects which are balloons, lasers, fireworks, shooting stars and confetti.

How to Send Digital Touch Messages

Digital Touch is a feature which allows you to send hand-drawn sketch, fireball, kiss, heartbeat or heartbreak.

1. On the left side of your text message box, tap the **arrow pointing to the right** (>) to open another set of cool effects.

2. You will see three icons which are the Camera, Digital Touch which looks like a heart and the button for syncing with third-party apps. Tap the **Digital Touch** icon. If you have started typing, it will be hidden until you tap the arrow to reveal the icons.

3. From here, you can see different effects that you can try. You can check out change the color of effects by tapping the circle on the left.

4. You can now draw your sketch or use one finger or two to create different effects like heartbeat.

5. Once finished, tap Send (blue up arrow).

How to Send Handwriting Message

Even if you can make a sketch of your messages in Digital Touch, there is also an added feature which allows you to handwrite your message.

1. Open Messages app and rotate your device to landscape mode. This will show you handwriting screen.

2. You can select from **previously sent** handwritten messages or write your new message with your finger.

3. Once finished, tap **Done**. You can also add more text if you need then tap the up arrow to send.

If you have to delete the handwritten message, you can always cancel it with the X icon or delete it with backspace key.

How to Enable Text Replacement and Keyboard Shortcuts

If you always need to type the same phrases or sentences all over again, you can always create keyboard shortcuts that will automatically transform into the whole phrase or sentences. This feature is beneficial since you no longer have to type everything all the time. For instance, instead of typing your whole address, you can make a short cut which will automatically enter your whole address.

1. Open **Settings** app from home screen.

2. Tap **Genera**l and select **Keyboard**.

3. Tap **Text Replacement**.

4. Tap the (+) sign to create keyboard shortcut and text replacement.

5. In the Phrase field, enter the whole phrase. (Example: Be Right Back)

6. In the Shortcut field, enter the shortcut you want to be replaced by the whole phrase. (Example: brb)

7. Once finished, tap **Save**.

You can create more keyboard shortcuts for the phrases that you often use. There are already premade shortcuts available in your device such as "omw" which becomes "On my way" after pressing the space bar.

How to Enable QuickType

QuickType feature predicts the words that you want to type. There is no need to type the whole word. After typing two letters, list of words will appear which you can just tap to use.

1. Open **Settings** app from home screen.

2. Tap **General** and go to **Keyboard**.

3. Toggle on **Predictive** feature.

Connect with Family and Friends using FaceTime

Apple devices have built-in app for audio and video calls which is FaceTime. This allows you to connect with your family and friends who are also using Apple devices. Once you register the contact number or e-mail of the person you want to contact and this person is also using an Apple device such as iPhone or iPad, you can easily connect with the person via FaceTime.

Before you start, make sure that you are connected to internet. The person that you wish to call via FaceTime should also have an active connection.

How to Turn On FaceTime

FaceTime is enabled automatically once you finished your startup process. However, if it is not activated, you can enable it manually.

1. Open **Setting** app from Home screen.
2. Tap **FaceTime**.
3. Tap to toggle on the switch beside FaceTime.

❑ How to Make Audio Call using FaceTime

You can use FaceTime app to make a regular call. Just make sure that you and the contact you wish to call have internet access.

1. From your Home screen, open **FaceTime** app.
2. Tap the name of the person you wish to call on the search bar.

3. Tap the **Phone** button which looks like a telephone to start the call.

❑ How to Make Video Call using FaceTime

1. From your Home screen, open **FaceTime** app.

2. Tap the name of the person you wish to call on the search bar.

3. Tap the **Video** button which looks like a camera.

❑ How to Block Contacts in FaceTime

You can also block contacts from FaceTime. Whether it is a prank caller or an annoying friend or your stalker, you can stop them from bothering you.

1. From your Home screen, open FaceTime app.

2. Search for the contact you wish to block then tap the information button (i).

3. Scroll down and tap Block this Caller.

4. Tap **Block Contact**.

❏ **Register Another Email Addresses for FaceTime**

1. Open **Settings** app from Home screen and tap FaceTime.

2. **Below You can be reached by FaceTime at** section, tap **Add Another Email...**

3. Type the email address you want to add.

4. Tap Back (< **Settings**).

How to Turn off FaceTime

1. Open **Settings** app from Home screen.

2. Tap **FaceTime**.

3. Tap to toggle off the switch beside FaceTime.

Enjoy the Advanced and Powerful Camera

The built-in Camera on iPhone 7 allows you to take true-life photos, videos, time-lapses, panoramas, slow motions and more. The camera of iPhone 7 as well as iPhone 7 plus are beyond all expectations. There are plenty of new features including 12 MP camera, 7MP

FaceTime HD camera, optical image stabilization and quad-LED true tone flash.

The **optical image stabilization** feature decreases the amount of blur from handshake or motion. There is a sensor which helps the lens to stabilize the movement for up to 3x longer exposure than iPhone 6s.

iPhone 7 camera's **f/1.8 aperture** allows more light to the sensor to increase its ability to take amazing low-light photos. It has **Quad-Led True Tone flash** which is 50 percent brighter compared to iPhone 6s.

❑ How to Access Camera Quickly

There are many ways to open the Camera app. Aside from tapping the Camera app, here are the other options on how to access camera quickly:

- The iOS 10 **lock screen** has new gesture which allows faster access to camera.

Step 1: Touch your lock screen.

Step 2: Swipe your finger to the left to access camera.

- You can access the Camera from **Control Center**.

Step 1: Swipe from the bottom of the screen to open Control Center.

Step 2: Tap the Camera button located on the bottom right.

Step 3: Hold the Camera button for a longer time to display different options which are Take Photo, Record Slo-Mo, Record Video and Take Selfie.

- You can use "**Hey Siri**" to open the Camera app and take photos, videos or selfie for you. All you need to do is to say the right command.

Step 1: Press and hold the Home button or say "Hey Siri" if you have turned on this feature.

Step 2: When Siri is activated, you can mentioned these phrases.

For photo mode:
- "Take a picture"
- "Take a Panoramic picture"
- "Take a square picture"

For video mode:
- "Take a video"
- "Take a Time-Lapse video"
- "Take a Slow-Motion video"

For selfie mode:
- "Take a selfie"

Step 3: Siri will launch the Camera app automatically. Now you take photos, videos or selfie by tapping the Circle button.

❏ How to Take Live Photos

Live photos are different from videos. It is a full 12 MP photo that can animate for 1.5 seconds. Live photos also work with iPhone SE, iPhone 6s, iPhone 6 Plus, iPhone 7, iPhone 7 plus and 9.7-inch iPad Pro. You can make your selfies live and powerful.

Step 1: Open the **Camera** app.

Step 2: Tap the **Live Photo** button. This looks like diffused rings. It should turn yellow once activated.

Step 3: Tap the **Circle** button to start your Live Photo.

❏ How to Lock Focus and Exposure

Step 1: Open the **Camera** app.

Step 2: Tap anywhere on the screen to select the part of the photo you wish to focus and expose.

Step 3: Tap and hold that area until AE/AF Lock banner appears on top of the screen.

Step 4: Tap the Circle or Shutter button to take a photo.

To unlock focus and exposure, simply tap anywhere.

❏ Bias Exposure

You can bias exposure to make photos darker or brighter.

Step 1: Open **Camera** app.

Step 2: Tap anywhere to enhance the focus point.

Step 3: Tap and hold the **Exposure** button which looks like a sun until you see a slider. This slider lets you make adjustments of the exposure.

Step 4: Simply drag the slider up or down to bias exposure. You can make your photos either brighter or even darker.

❏ How to Use Grid Lines

If you want some help from grid lines for taking pictures, you can enable grid lines from Settings app.

Step 1: Open **Settings** app.

Step 2: Scroll down and select **Photos & Camera**.

Step 3: Scroll down until you see the Camera section. Toggle on the switch of **Grid**.

3

MUSIC, NOTES AND SIRI

Listen to Millions of Songs with Music App

There are four ways to get music on your new iPhone 7. You can easily purchase music directly from the iTunes Store, use iTunes Match with a fee of £21.99 per year, use iCloud Music Library or Sync music from iTunes using your Mac or PC.

How to Sync Music from iTunes on PC or Mac

1. Connect your device to your Mac or PC via lightning cable.

2. Launch **iTunes**.

3. Click your device located in the top-left of the screen.

4. Select **Music** from the sidebar.

5. Click **Sync Music**.

6. It will sync your whole music library. If you do not want to sync all the songs from your iTunes library, simply put ticks next to the Playlists, Albums, Genres and Artists.

7. Click **Apply**. All music that you selected will be synced to your device.

How to Use Music App

1. Open **Music** app from home screen.

2. You will see many options below the screen. If you did not take the Apple Music subscription yet, you will see: Library, For You, Browse, Radio and Search.

3. Tap **Library** to stream the music you added on your iPhone. You can select from Playlists, Artists, Albums, Songs and Downloaded Music.

4. Tap any song to start. It will show you the **Now Playing** interface. Simply tap the left and right

arrows to switch songs. You can also tap **Repeat** or **Shuffle** button located at the bottom.

Subscribe to Apple Music

You can listen to almost all tracks in iTunes Store when you subscribe to Apple Music. You also get three months free trial. If you want to get a subscription, simply open the **Music** app and tap **For You**. Then tap **Start three Month Free Trial**. Another way to subscribe is from **Settings** app. Select **Music** then tap **Show Apple Music**.

Access Your Notes Anytime, Anywhere

Notes app is one of the most used apps on iPhone. It allows you to type anything that you like. Now, you can also make sketches so you can save your visual ideas next to your texts. There are different format and styles that you can choose from. You can also use numbered and bulleted list when necessary.

Photos, videos, audio, website links, documents and locations can also be added in your Notes app so you can keep everything that you need accordingly. You can use Notes app for almost everything from work to your shopping list. You can take some notes on your iPhone and continue it later on your Mac.

Create and Edit New Notes

1. Open **Notes** app.

2. Tap **Create New Note** button from the bottom right.

3. Tap the screen to show the keyboard and you can start to take down notes.

4. To create another note, simply tap the **New Note** button.

5. To edit existing notes, tap the note you wish to edit then tap anywhere to show the keyboard.

Move a Note to a New Folder

If you have many notes and you want to organize them by creating folders, you can do it easily.

1. Open **Notes** app.

2. Tap the existing folder where your note is saved.

3. Tap **Edit** from the upper right beside the name of the folder.

4. Tap the circle next to your note then tap **Move to...** in the bottom.

5. Choose a folder where you wish to transfer your note to.

How to Delete and Recover Deleted Notes

To delete a note, simply tap the note you wish to delete then tap the **Trashcan** button in the bottom. Another way is to tap the title of the note then swipe it to the left to show two options: Move and Delete. Tap **Delete**.

If you want to recover your deleted notes, go to list view screen and tap Back button to display a list of folders. Tap **Recently Deleted** and look for the note that you want to recover. Swipe it to the left and tap **Move** to transfer it back to your folder.

Enable Notes Sync with iCloud

To sync your notes with iCloud, follow these steps:

1. Open **Settings** app on your iPhone or iPad.

2. Select **iCloud**.

3. Enter your email address and password. Tap **Sign in**.

4. Enable Notes sync. Make sure that it is green.

Set Password on your Notes

You can set a password on your Notes to keep it private even when someone has to borrow your iDevice. There are two ways to lock your notes.

Lock Notes from Notes app:

1. Open **Notes** app from Home screen.

2. Tap a note that you want to lock then tap the **Share** button.

3. Tap **Lock Note** option to lock it.

4. Enter your **Password** which you will use for all your notes in your iDevices. Enter your password again.

5. You can add a hint if necessary.

6. If you want to unlock your notes easier, you can switch to **Touch ID** which can unlock your notes using your fingerprint.

Lock Notes from Settings app:

1. Open **Settings** app from home screen.

2. Tap **Notes**.

3. Tap **Password**.

4. Enter your **Password** which you will use for all your notes in your iDevices. Enter your password again.

5. You can add a hint if necessary.

6. If you want to unlock your notes easier, you can switch to **Touch ID** which can unlock your notes using your fingerprint.

Note: The entire body of the note will not be visible when locked but the title is in order to make it easier for you to find them. To keep all information hidden, make sure to avoid any info in the title.

How to Change Password on Notes

Changing passwords can be necessary from time to time.

1. Open **Settings** app then tap **Notes**.

2. Tap **Password** then select **Change Password**.

3. Enter your **Old Password**.

4. Enter your **New Password** and enter your new password again to confirm.

5. You can add a hint if necessary.

6. Once finished, tap **Done**.

How to Unlock Notes

Your locked notes will remain hidden except for the title. To unlock your notes, follow these steps:

1. Open **Notes** app from Home screen.

2. Tap the note you wish to unlock.

3. Tap **View Note** or the **Lock** icon.

4. Enter your password or use Touch ID if you activated this feature.

Siri: Get More Things Done

Siri is one of the most awesome features of Apple devices. You can complete your tasks faster with the help of Siri. You can ask questions like the how's the weather, latest movies in Netflix, nearby restaurants, new songs, stocks and more. You can command Siri to call someone, set a reminder, turn on timer, play songs, make reservations, read mails, create notes and calculate. There are more things that Siri can do for you.

After the release of iOS 10, Siri has become smarter than ever which can do almost everything you command from simple opening of apps to searching of information. Whether you are driving or cooking, you can command your smartphone using your voice.

How to Activate "Hey Siri"

You can command Siri without having to hold your iPhone by activating "Hey Siri" feature. This feature works when your device is connected to a power.

1. Open **Settings** app.
2. Tap **Siri**.
3. Turn on **Siri**.
4. Turn on "**Hey Siri**".
5. Follow the onscreen instructions which will ask you to speak "Hey Siri" three times and "How's the weather today."

When your iPhone is connected to charger, you can simply say Hey Siri and the Siri interface will open automatically. You can dismiss Siri by saying "**see you later**" or just "**bye**."

Siri Now Works for Other Apps

Siri is now integrated with other apps which means that there are more things that you can do easily. Siri works with these types of apps:

- Messaging
- CarPlay
- Ride booking
- VoIP calling
- Photo and Video
- Payment
- Workouts

You can ask Siri which apps can work. If the app does not, Siri will tell you, "I wish I could, but (name of the app) hasn't set that up with me yet."

Siri is also working in the background by giving suggestions. For instance, Siri can make a calendar event depending on the conversation in email or iMessage. If you ask someone if they want to go out for dinner, Siri can make suggestions of nearby restaurants. It also makes suggestions on keyboard which is known as the **QuickType** feature.

4

PASSCODE AND TOUCH ID

Set Passcode on Your iPhone

Setting a passcode on your iPhone prevents anyone from unlocking your device as they need to enter numbers to unlock it first. This means that it will be hard for your friends or anyone to check your private photos, messages, health and financial information.

How to Set Passcode

1. Open **Settings** app from home screen.

2. Select **Touch ID & Passcode**.

3. Tap **Turn Passcode On**.

4. Enter your passcode and re-enter passcode to confirm.

Change Passcode

If you want to change passcode, you can always do so.

1. Open **Settings** app from home screen.

2. Select **Touch ID & Passcode**.

3. Enter your current passcode.

4. Select **Change Passcode**.

5. Re-enter your current passcode.

6. Enter your new passcode. Re-enter to confirm.

How to Switch to Alphanumeric Passcode

If you prefer more complicated passcode but not long enough that you might not remember, alphanumeric can be your choice.

1. Open **Settings** app from home screen.

2. Select **Touch ID & Passcode**.

3. Enter your current passcode.

4. Tap **Change Passcode** and re-enter your current passcode.

5. Tap **Passcode Options** and select **Custom Alphanumeric Code**.

6. Enter your new alphanumeric password. Re-enter to confirm.

How to Turn Passcode Off

It is recommended to keep your passcode on. If you need to turn passcode off, here's what to do.

1. Open **Settings** app from home screen.

2. Select **Touch ID & Passcode**.

3. Enter your current passcode.

4. Tap **Turn Passcode Off** and confirm.

5. Re-enter your passcode to turn off.

Touch ID: More Convenient Way to Unlock Device

Touch ID is your device's sensor in the Home button to identify your fingerprint. This is one form of security which is more convenient than having to enter your passcode. Since you always use your iPhone, you will need to unlock it every now and then. Typing your password all the time can be inconvenient at times. Touch ID allows you to unlock your screen faster.

❑ **How to Set Up Touch ID**

During the initial set up, you were asked to register your fingerprint. You can also add more fingers any time you want to.

1. Open **Settings** app from home screen.

2. Tap **Touch ID & Passcode**.

3. Type your passcode to confirm. Entering passcode requires Touch ID and if you do not have it yet, you will be prompted to create.

4. Tap **Add a Fingerprint** button.

5. Place the **finger** you wish to register on **Home button** until it vibrates.

6. Raise your finger then put it back on Home button every time you feel the vibration.

7. When it prompts that it has finished the first step and requires peripheral data, tap **Continue**.

8. Put the edges of the finger you wish to register on the Home button. Leave it until it vibrates.

9. Raise your finger then put it back on Home button. Repeat using the other edge of your finger until the entire surface is registered.

10. Once finished, tap **Continue**.

You can add more fingers by repeating all the steps above. You can allow your family members' fingerprint or someone you really trust.

❏ How to Rename Touch ID Fingerprints

You can put names on your fingerprint so you would not have to identify which fingers are already registered. For instance, you can name it "right thumb" if you registered your right thumb.

1. Open **Settings** app.

2. Tap **Touch ID & Passcode**.

3. Enter your passcode when prompted.

4. Tap the finger you wish to rename.

5. Enter the name that is more convenient for you to identify.

5. Once finished, tap **Done**.

❑ How to Delete Touch ID Fingerprint

If you allowed someone to gain access to your iPhone for a short period of time and there is no need for that person to have an access to your device, you can easily delete their fingerprint.

1. Open **Settings** app from home screen.

2. Select **Touch ID & Passcode**.

3. Enter your passcode when asked.

4. Select the **fingerprint** you wish to delete.

5. Tap **Delete Fingerprint** then tap **Done** to finish.

❑ How to Disable Touch ID for iPhone Unlock

Touch ID allows you to unlock your device faster. If you prefer typing alphanumeric for stronger password, you can disable Touch ID.

1. Open **Settings** app from home screen.

2. Select **Touch ID & Passcode**.

3. Enter your passcode when asked.

4. Toggle off **iPhone Unlock**.

❑ **How to Disable Touch ID for Apple Pay**

Touch ID is required for Apple Pay. If you prefer to enter your passcode, simply disable Touch ID for Apple Pay.

1. Open **Settings** app.

2. Select **Touch ID & Passcode**.

3. Enter your passcode when asked.

4. Toggle off **Apple Pay**.

❑ **How to Disable Touch ID for iTunes and App Store**

If you prefer typing your password on iTunes and App Store than using Touch ID, you can also turn it off.

1. Open **Settings** app.

2. Select **Touch ID & Passcode**.

3. Enter your passcode when asked.

4. Toggle off **iTunes & App Store**.

❏ **Cases when Touch ID Turns Off Automatically**

There are cases that Touch ID turns off automatically to secure your files and information.

- When Touch ID has not been used in forty eight hours.
- When your devices has been reset or rebooted.
- When fingerprint is not recognized five times in a row.
- When passcode has not been used to unlock in 6 days.
- When a remote lock has been sent using Find My iPhone.

You will have to enter your passcode again to activate Touch ID.

5

3D TOUCH AND AIRPLAY

Make Quick Actions with 3D Touch
3D Touch allows you to press the display in order to do more with your games and other apps. You can move around and complete tasks even faster. You can activate trackpad mode using 3D touch and also animate your live photos.

Home Screen Actions with 3D Touch

There are many actions available from your home screen. All you have to do is to press firmly.

1. From Home screen, press firmly on an **icon** you wish to open quick actions for.

2. A list of actions will be displayed. Tap the action that you need.

Switch Apps with 3D Touch

You can easily switch apps using 3D touch.

1. Press firmly on the left side of your screen.

2. Swipe to the right to see previous apps and swipe more to the right to show fast app switcher.

3. Swipe to the app you wish to open then tap that app.

Check and Clear Notifications with 3D Touch

You can check and interact with your notifications using 3D touch. From lock screen, simply swipe to the right to see Notification Center.

1. Press a notification you want to interact with.

2. You can type and interact with the notification.

3. To disregard the notification, simply tap the X button.

3D touch also allows you to clean your Notification Center by deleting all notifications. To do this:

1. Press the **X** button on top of the notifications.
2. Tap **Clear All Notifications**.

Peek and Pop

3D Touch allows you to peek and pop messages, automatic links and website links. Peek allows you to perform certain actions without opening the app.

1. Press the link or item you wish to peek at.
2. The link or item will be highlighted while the rest of your screen will become blurred.
3. To peek at the item or link, simply press firmly.
4. Once finished, you can let go to release the peek.
5. For more actions, simply swipe up from the item or link to show the list.
6. Select the action you wish to perform.

To pop a message and show it in your entire screen:

1. Press the message to peek.

2. To make it pop, press longer.

3. To go back to the previous app, simply tap the Back button or press hard on the left side of the screen then swipe to the right.

How to Customize 3D Touch

If you want to change the sensitivity level of your 3D touch, it is easy to do so.

1. Open **Settings** app from home screen.

2. Select **General**.

3. Tap **Accessibility** and select **3D Touch**.

4. There are three levels that you can choose from: **light**, **medium** and **firm**.

5. Select your desired sensitivity level.

How to Turn Off 3D Touch

If you prefer to disable 3D touch, you can easily do so.

1. Open **Settings** app from home screen.

2. Select **General**.

3. Tap **Accessibility** and select **3D Touch**.

4. Toggle off 3D Touch.

AirPlay: Stream Photos, Videos, Movies and Music to Apple TV

AirPlay can only be used when there is an active connection. Once you connect all your devices that are compatible with AirPlay to the same internet connection, you can stream your videos or music on Apple TV or AirPlay Speaker. You can enjoy movies on bigger screen or mirror your entire iPhone screen.

❏ How to Use AirPlay Video

1. To use AirPlay, open **Control Center** by swiping up from the bottom of the screen.

2. Tap the **AirPlay** button.

3. Tap to confirm and your iPhone 7 will start searching for an Apple TV.

4. If the Apple TV you want to use has different network from your iPhone, it will show a code which you have to enter on your iPhone.

❑ How to Stop AirPlay Video

1. To end AirPlay video, open **Control Center** by swiping up from the bottom of the screen.
2. Tap the **AirPlay** button.
3. Tap **Turn Off AirPlay Mirroring**.

❑ How to Use AirPlay Audio

1. To stream your music to Apple TV or AirPlay speakers, open **Control Center** by swiping up from the bottom of the screen.
2. Swipe to the left to open **Now Playing** screen.
3. Select **Audio Destination** and choose the device where you want to stream your music.

❑ How to Stop AirPlay Audio

1. To stop AirPlay audio, simply go to **Control Center** by swiping up from the bottom of the screen.

2. Swipe from right to left top open **Now Playing** screen.

3. Tap the **Audio Destination** button and select iPhone to discontinue AirPlay.

6

TWO-FACTOR AUTHENTICATION AND ICLOUD KEYCHAIN

Two-Factor Authentication for Additional Security

The security of your information is one of the things that have to be given importance. For more security of your iCloud account and your Apple ID, Apple released two-factor authentication feature. This feature provides an extra layer of protection for all your accounts. You can only use this feature only on the devices that you trust so there is no way other people can gain access to your information.

When two-factor authentication feature is enabled, you will have to enter your password plus a six-digit verification code when logging in to a different or new device. This only means that if someone tries to sign in your account from their devices, they cannot succeed even if they were able to know your first password.

How Two-Factor Authentication Works

Two-factor authentication only works on all devices that you trusted such as your iPhone, iPad and your Mac. If you have to sign in on your new device, you will need to enter a six-digit code which will be displayed on your trusted devices. First, you need to enter the six-digit code on your trusted devices to confirm that the new device is also trusted. This means that your first password is not enough to get your account. Two-factor authentication can make your information double secured.

How to Turn On Two-Factor Authentication

1. Open **Settings** app from home screen.

2. Select **iCloud**.

3. Tap **Apple ID** and enter your password when asked.

4. Select **Password & Security**.

5. Enable **Two-Factor Authentication**.

6. Tap **Continue** and follow the given instructions from your screen.

Once the two-factor authentication is on, you will need to verify yourself when signing in to iCloud or Apple ID page. You also need to confirm when making purchases from iBooks, App Store and iTunes using new devices. iMessage, Game Center and FaceTime are also covered by two-factor authentication.

Keep Passwords and Usernames with iCloud Keychain

You can keep your usernames and passwords for Safari, credit card and Wi-Fi network up to date for all your iOS devices and Mac. It is secured with 256-bit AES encryption. iCloud Keychain can be used with Safari Password Generator and AutoFill. You can use AutoFill to let your device enter your account information automatically. To keep your information secured, you have to set a passcode when enabling iCloud Keychain and AutoFill.

1. To set up **iCloud Keychain**, open **Settings** app from home screen.

2. Tap **iCloud** then select **Keychain**.

3. Toggle on **iCloud Keychain**.

4. Follow the instructions onscreen.

During the set up, you need to create a security code to authorize your other devices in using iCloud Keychain.

7

REMINDERS AND APP STORE

Never Forget with Reminder App
You can always ask Siri to make a reminder for you. But if you prefer to manually create your reminder and organize everything yourself, it is easy to navigate the Reminder app. You can also choose the priorities of your reminders.

How to Create a Reminder

1. Open the **Reminders** app.
2. Tap the (+) icon to create a reminder.

3. Enter your reminder on the space provided then tap (**i**).

4. You can enable either "**Remind me on a day**" or "**Remind me at a location**". Remind me at a location gives you a reminder when you arrive or leave from your chosen location.

5. Choose the **priority** of your reminder. You can select from one exclamation mark to three exclamation marks.

6. To add notes on your reminder, simply tap **Notes** under Priority.

7. Tap **Done** to save your reminder.

Download Apps and Games from App Store

There are millions of games and apps that you can download to your device. You can download Facebook app directly to your device so it is just one tap away. Edit your documents anytime and anywhere. Play millions of games whether online or offline. There are many apps to discover. The categories of apps in App Store are:

- Books
- Business
- Catalogues
- Education
- Entertainment
- Finance
- Food & Drink
- Games
- Health & Fitness
- Kids
- Lifestyle
- Magazines & Newspapers
- Medical
- Music
- Navigation
- News
- Photo & Video
- Productivity
- Shopping
- Social Networking
- Sports
- Travel
- Utilities
- Weather

How to Search and Download Games and Apps

Once you have an Apple ID, you can make start downloading games and other apps from App Store.

1. Open **App Store**.

2. Tap the **Search** button at the bottom of your screen.

3. Enter the name of app that you want to download.

4. Tap **Search**. When the results appeared, tap **Get** if the app is free or the **price** if it is paid app then tap **Install**.

Update Your Apps

Developers always release new updates to keep the apps glitches-free. To check if there are new updates:

1. Open **App Store**.

2. Tap **Updates**.

3. All apps with new updates are available to install. Simply tap the **Update** button of the apps you wish to update.

Update Apps Automatically

You can update your apps automatically without having to open App Store.

1. Open **Settings** app.

2. Select **iTunes & App Store**.

3. Tap the switch next to **Updates** under Automatic Downloads. This will automatically update your apps when connected to internet.

From here, you can also enable automatic downloads for Books & Audiobooks, Apps and Music.

How to Disable Updates When Using Cellular

To avoid using cellular data from updating apps, it is best turn off automatic update for Cellular Data.

1. Open **Settings** app from home screen.

2. Select **iTunes & App Store**.

3. Toggle off the switch next to **Use Cellular Data**.

8

PERSONALIZE, AIRDROP AND BATTERY

Personalize Your iPhone

You can easily personalize your iPhone.

Arrange Apps

To arrange your apps, simply tap and hold the app from your home screen until all apps are jiggling. Drag the app that you wish to move. You can also transfer your apps from different home screen by dragging the app to the edge of the screen.

To delete apps from your home screen, tap the **X** button on top of the app. You can also delete some of the built-in Apple apps such as Calculator, Calendar, Compass, Contacts, FaceTime, Home, Podcasts, Reminders, Stocks, Voice Memos, Watch, Weather and more.

You can create a folder of your apps by dragging one app to another app. Tap the name of the folder to change its name. To save your app arrangement, simply tap the Home button.

Change Wallpaper

To change your wall paper, go to Settings > Wallpaper > Choose a New Wallpaper. You can also use your own image for your wallpaper.

To set a Live Photo as your wall paper for lock screen, go to Settings > Wallpaper > Choose New Wallpaper. From there, tap Live and choose your live photo. When you are on your lock screen, you can press to watch your live photo.

Adjust Screen Brightness

Low brightness or auto-brightness feature can conserve your battery life. You can use Night Shift to make your screen warmer during the night. To adjust the brightness of your screen, go to Settings then tap Display & Brightness. Drag the slider to adjust. Screen brightness can also be adjusted from the Control Center.

Change iPhone Name

If you want to use your change the name of your iPhone, go to Settings and tap General. Select About. Tap Name.

Share Your Files with AirDrop

AirDrop allows you to share your files such as photos, videos, locations, websites and other items with other devices running iOS 7 or later. AirDrop requires an active internet connection and Bluetooth to transfer the files. You also have to sign in to your iCloud.

To share files using AirDrop, simply select the photo or video you wish to share. Tap the share button then select the name of the person you want to share the files with.

To receive AirDrop files from others, all you have to do is to enable AirDrop and Bluetooth from Control Center. Once the request arrives, tap Accept.

How to Enhance iPhone 7 Battery Life

The battery life of iPhone 7 as well as iPhone 7 plus is already improved. It is longer than its predecessors. iPhone 7 is packed with new awesome features with enhanced performances. It includes improved camera features. If you want to make the battery life of your device longer, these are some tips that you can do.

❑ Turn on Low Power Mode

The iPhone 7 comes with a feature Low Power Mode which can help your battery to last even longer. Low Power Mode prompts automatically once your battery reaches 20% and you can enable it by then. But if you want to turn it on even if you still have 100%, you may do so.

When Low Power Mode is on, it stops all apps running in the background. It also stops fetching new data to conserve the battery.

1. Launch **Settings** app.

2. Tap **Battery**.

3. Turn on **Low Power Mode**.

❑ **Turn On Auto Brightness**

Auto Brightness feature adjusts the screen brightness automatically. When your surroundings are bright, your screen will become brighter so you can see your screen well. Once it is night time or you are already in bed, your screen automatically lowers its brightness which can help in conserving your device's battery life.

1. Open **Settings** app.

2. Tap **Display & Brightness**.

3. Toggle on **Auto Brightness**.

❏ **Disable Push Notification**

Push notifications for mails and calendar contribute to draining your battery life fast. You can disable this feature if you do not need push notification. You can always open your app to check for new data.

1. Open **Settings** app from home screen.

2. Tap **Notifications**.

3. Toggle off **Push** notifications for apps that you do not need Push.

❏ **Disable Location Services**

When not using location services, it is best to turn it off. Location service is a great feature and can consume battery life as well. You can always turn it back on when needed such as when using Google Maps or Waze.

1. Launch **Settings** app from home screen.

2. Select **Privacy**.

3. Toggle off **Location Services**.

When using Google Maps or other apps that require location, you can easily turn it back on by repeating the same steps then toggle on Location Services. Once finished with the feature, turn it back off to conserve the battery life of your device.

❏ **Turn Off Background App Refresh**

Your device will keep the apps running in the background. Even if you are using a different app, the previous apps you used and you did not close will continue consuming your battery. It collects data and information in the background in order to keep you updated even without having to open the app. With feature on, there is no need to refresh the apps. However, if you need to conserve your battery, it is best to turn this feature off. To turn off background app refresh feature:

1. Open **Settings** app from home screen.

2. Tap **General**.

3. Scroll down and select **Background App Refresh**.

4. Turn off the switch to discontinue apps in the background from collecting new data.

9

BASIC TROUBLESHOOTING SOLUTIONS

Perform Basic Troubleshooting Solutions

If you are experiencing some problems with your iPhone 7, learn what to do:

Touch ID Stopped Working

If Touch ID stopped working, follow these steps:

1. Go to **Settings** and tap **Touch ID & Passcode**.
2. Enter your passcode. Toggle **off** the switches next to iTunes & Apple Store and Apple Pay.

3. **Reboot** your iPhone and wait for few minutes before turning it back on.

4. Turn **on** your device and go back to Settings.

5. Toggle **on** the switches next to iTunes & Apple Store and Apple Pay.

The alternative solution is to delete fingerprints that you registered. Follow these steps:

1. Open **Settings** app and select **Touch ID & Passcode**.

2. Turn **off** each item then tap **Delete Fingerprint**.

3. **Add A Fingerprint** again and turn back **on** all items.

iMessage Not Working

iMessage only works when there is an active connection such as Wi-Fi and 3G network. Make sure that your device is connected to internet when using iMessage. Here are some solutions that you can do:

1. **Turn off iMessage**. Do this by going to Settings > Messages > iMessage. Turn it back on after few minutes and make sure you are connected to 3G or Wi-Fi.

2. **Reboot your device**. Press and hold down Sleep/Wake button until the slider appears. Swipe the slider to turn off. Wait for few seconds before turning your devices on.

3. **Toggle on and off Airplane mode**. Go to Settings > Airplane Mode.

4. **Reset Network Settings**. To reset network settings, open Settings > General > Reset > Reset Network Settings. After resetting, you will need to connect your device again to Wi-Fi and enter the password.

iMessage Effects Not Working

iMessage is packed with new features. There are bubble and screen effects that you can use to improve your iMessaging experience. If the effects are not working, learn what to do.

Turn off Reduce Motion. Go to Settings app and tap General. Select Accessibility and look for Reduce Motion. Make sure that Reduce Motion feature is off to enable bubble and screen effects on iMessage.

iMessage Handwriting Feature Not Working

You can easily access handwriting screen in Messages app by tilting your device to landscape mode. If it does not appear, simply tap Handwriting feature button which looks like a small loop. This will show the handwriting space. To go back to keyboard, simply tap the keyboard button.

Device Cannot Connect to Wi-Fi

If experiencing Wi-Fi grayed out, you can try some of the solutions below:

1. **Disable Wi-Fi Settings.** Go to Settings, tap Privacy and select Location Services. Tap System Services then look for Wi-Fi Networking. Turn off Wi-Fi Networking.

2. **Restart your iPhone**. Press and hold down Sleep/Wake button until the slider appears. Swipe the slider to turn off your device. Turn your device back on and try to connect to Wi-Fi.

3. **Reset Network Settings**. To reset network settings, open Settings > General > Reset > Reset Network Settings. After resetting, you will need to connect your device again to Wi-Fi and enter the password.

Apps Not Producing Sounds

If there are no sounds when opening your apps, here are the solutions to fix the issue.

1. **Check Mute Switch**. The mute switch is on the left side of the device. Make sure that the switch is

not showing orange. If it shows orange, it means your device is muted.

2. **Turn off Bluetooth**. Your device can still be connected to Bluetooth speaker or headset. Switch off Bluetooth by swiping up from the bottom of the screen to open Control Center. Turn Bluetooth off.

3. **Disable Do Not Disturb**. Open Control Center and tap the moon sign to turn off Do Not Disturb feature. When this feature is on, it prevents your device from making any sound.

4. **Check Volume Setting.** The volume setting of your device can be on zero which results to your apps not producing sounds. Open the app you are having problems with and press the volume button at the side of your device.

5. **Reset All Settings**. To reset, open Settings > General > Reset > Reset All Settings.

How to Remove "Press Home Button to Unlock"

If you do not want to press the Home button to unlock your device, you can enable Rest Finger to Open. You do not actually press the Home button. It is just a haptic feedback which gives the feeling of pressing the button. To disable the haptic feedback, go to **Settings** > **General** > **Accessibility** > **Home Button** then toggle on **Rest Finger to Open**.

FaceTime Not Working

FaceTime works when there is an active connection. Make sure that your device is connected to Wi-Fi or 3G to use it. If it still does not work, try some of the solutions below.

1. **Get the Latest Update of iOS**. Make sure that you have installed the new update of iOS. Go to Settings, tap General and select Software Update. If your device is up to date, check more solutions below.

2. **Check if FaceTime is on**. Make sure that FaceTime is toggled on in Settings. To check, open Settings app and scroll down to FaceTime. Make sure that it is on or it is green.

3. **Reactivate your account**. Open Settings and tap FaceTime. Turn it off and wait for a minute before turning it back on. Enter your Apple ID and password.

4. **Reboot your device**. To reboot your device, hold down the Sleep/Wake button together with the Volume down button until the Apple logo appears. Once on, try to connect to FaceTime again.

5. **Use Same Apple ID**. Make sure that your Apple ID is the same as your FaceTime account. To check, open Settings app and tap FaceTime.

6. **Toggle on and off Airplane mode**. Go to Settings and toggle on and off Airplane Mode.

7. **Reset Network Settings**. To reset network settings, open Settings > General > Reset > Reset Network Settings. After resetting, you will need to connect your device again to Wi-Fi and enter the password.

Keyboard Landscape Mode Not Functioning

You can easily switch to landscape mode on keyboard when you tilt your device. If landscape mode does not appear, here are some solutions that you can do.

1. **Turn your device off and on**. Once on, go to Messages app and tilt your keyboard. Landscape mode should appear instantly.

2. **Disable Turn to Listen**. Another solution that can be done is to go to Settings and tap Messages. Turn off Raise to Listen.

Bluetooth Not Working with Other Devices

If having problems with Bluetooth, know what to do:

1. **Turn Bluetooth off.** Go to Settings and turn off Bluetooth. Reboot your device by holding the Sleep/Wake button and Volume down button until the Apple logo appears. When your device is on, turn Bluetooth on and connect it to your other device.

2. **Forget This Device.** Another solution is to forget the device you want to connect. Go to Settings and tap Bluetooth. Tap the information button (i) next to the device name. Tap "Forget This Device" and confirm. Try to pair again with the device and it should work.

3. **Reset Network Settings.** To reset network settings, open Settings > General > Reset > Reset Network Settings. After resetting, you will need to connect your device again to Wi-Fi and enter the password.

iPhone 7 is one of the most advanced gadgets available in the market today. It is packed with cool features that can make your daily tasks easier while enjoying your smartphone experience. It is your all-in-one device which allows you to take real-life photos, connect to your family and friends anytime and anywhere, install apps that you need and more. You can easily command Siri to make actions for you.

Conclusion

I hope this guide has helped you understand more about the phone in details. Wishing you all the best and good luck!

36163329R00054

Made in the USA
Middletown, DE
26 October 2016